How the Republican Party Became Pro-Life

Phyllis Schlafly

Permission to quote in critical reviews with citation:
How the Republican Party Became Pro-Life
By Phyllis Schlafly

ISBN 978-0-9884613-9-0

www.dunrobin.us

TABLE OF CONTENTS

Foreword by Bob Novak   i
Chapter 1: First Skirmishes   1
Chapter 2: 1976 – Starting Republicans on a New Road   8
Chapter 3: 1980 – Pro-Life Republicans Make Waves   12
Chapter 4: 1984 – Locking Pro-Life Into the Platform   19
Chapter 5: 1988 – Let the Good Times Roll   22
Chapter 6: 1992 – The Year of the Red Cowboy Hats   25
Chapter 7: 1996 – Don't Change a Comma   33
Chapter 8: 2000 – Pro-Life Becomes the *Life* of the Party   41
Chapter 9: 2004 – Sticking By Our Principles   43
Chapter 10: 2008 – Overcoming Unexpected Problems   45
Chapter 11: 2012 – America is Becoming Pro-Life   48
Chapter 12: Rejecting Judicial Supremacy   52
Afterword by Kristan Hawkins   58
Appendix A: Pro-Life References in Republican Platforms   60
Appendix B: Pro-Marriage References in Republican Platforms   76
Appendix C: We Believe in America 2012 Republican Platform   87
Appendix D: Resolutions Passed by the RNC   94
About the Author   131

Foreword by Bob Novak

The first I ever heard of Phyllis Schlafly was in 1964 when she published *A Choice Not an Echo*. She was a housewife from Alton, Illinois, forty years old, and I was a budding columnist. The late Roland Evans and I had just started our column in 1963. In 1964, I was a 33-year-old syndicated columnist. I read the book and I thought it was one of the best-written, most interesting, fascinating pieces of political advocacy that I had ever read in my life. And I wouldn't say I disagreed with everything in it, but damn near everything.

Now, I am in the process of writing my memoirs and I came across a copy of the book in the process and I sat down and read it all the way through ... I couldn't stop. And you know, forty years later, I agree with almost everything in it.

I tell people that I have had a long journey to the right and I say I get a little more Conservative every day. And they say, well there's no more room on the right for you to go. (Pointing at Phyllis): Well, yes there is! I agree with Phyllis on almost everything now, but not everything. I'm working at it. And I hope I'll get there. She had been very important in guiding me to the right, which has been incremental and not sudden.

She's also been important in guiding somebody to the right who she may have met but she doesn't really know, and that's my wife. My wife, Geraldine, would die if she knew I was going to mention her name. She is one of the most private people I've ever met. When I met this Texas girl, she had never met a Republican until she was a grown woman. When I first met her in 1960, she was one of Sen. Lyndon Johnson's secretaries, a registered Democrat, and when I married her in 1962, she was Vice President Johnson's secretary. She has, in the course of time, changed her registration from Democrat to Republican. She has spent the last many years as a behind-the-scenes, fervent, pro-life activist. And she has been guided, although Phyllis didn't know it, by Phyllis Schlafly, all those years.

So, I thank Phyllis, and I also thank God for what has been a wonderful journey over these forty years. Because I say, it's been a great life for me, covering politics, making politicians uncomfortable, saying whatever I want to say, writing whatever I want to write. What a great country and what a great privilege that has been for me.

One of my favorite things over the years has been covering Republican platform hearings ... and watching Phyllis Schlafly in action at these hearings. It is awesome! Here is a person who holds no public office, usually not a party position, doesn't run a big lobbying firm, doesn't represent a big corporation or a special interest group, and she instills awe, fear, respect, and she has influence. I really do believe, that as Faith Whittlesey said, that the Republican Party, remaining a pro-life party, would not have been possible all these years if it had not been for the work at these platform hearings and sessions of Phyllis Schlafly. Because, presidential candidates, and even incumbent presidents (we won't name names) wanted to bail out on that issue, on many occasions, I can guarantee you.

iii

At the last hearing, the last session of the platform committee at the Jacob Javits building in New York ... she was really awesome. People in the White House pulled for most of the members of the platform committee - even governors and wives... some little aide at the White House would say something and they would just collapse. But Phyllis has principles. And she, I believe, has not only influenced the draft of the platform, but she influenced how the changes were made. Did she win everything? Absolutely not. But she, believe me, was the only force from the outside that had any influence because all the platform committee members wanted to do was get along with the White House.

I would suppose everybody in this room, or nearly everybody, is for George W. Bush's re-election. I would certainly hope so. But I believe it is part of the Conservative movement and part of being an American that you don't salam when the people in power say you have to do something and Phyllis Schlafly has led the way on that.

Statement made by Bob Novak at Phyllis Schlafly's 80th Birthday on September 18, 2004

First Skirmishes

Abortion law had traditionally been in the domain of the states, as was nearly all criminal law. Beginning in 1967, more than a dozen states weakened in various ways their laws that made abortion a crime. This movement was made easier because, in the 1960s, conventional wisdom told Americans that the earth was running out of food and we would face mass starvation when the earth could no longer feed our growing population. The implication was that people would be doing a good thing if they limited births.

This fallacy was promoted by the two-million-copy sale of the 1968 book called *The Population Bomb* by college professor Paul R. Ehrlich. I remember attending a dinner party hosted by a prominent neighbor who solemnly warned us that this might be our last roast beef dinner because America would soon be unable to afford to raise cattle for food.

1

Conventional concern about a worldwide problem of overpopulation and our duty to "do something" to save ourselves from a terrible fate reached the White House during the presidency of Richard Nixon. The United States Agency for International Development (USAID) began to spend millions on the "problem" of overpopulation.

On December 26, 1970, Nixon signed the Family Planning Services and Population Research Act (better known as Title X) creating a national commitment to provide adequate family planning services to all Americans who wanted them but couldn't afford them. This legislation on family planning and population had strong bipartisan support.

When Nixon sent this legislation to Congress, in 1969, he warned about the increasing rate of population growth and predicted that by the year 2000 the Earth would have eight billion people. To implement a national commitment to limit our population, Nixon asked for expanded research in contraceptive development. The National Center for Family Planning Services was established in what was then called the Department of Health, Education and Welfare.

The pro-abortion momentum was stalled by a defeat in the Illinois Legislature in 1969. However, in 1970, Planned Parenthood of New York City started the battle to legalize abortion in New York State. The tide of public opinion turned against abortion in 1971. Pro-abortion bills failed to pass in any state in 1971 and 1972. The New York legislature even repealed its two-year-old abortion-on-demand law (only to have the repeal vetoed by Governor Nelson Rockefeller). In November 1972, pro-abortion referenda were defeated by the voters in North Dakota with a 77 percent vote and in Michigan by a 61 percent vote.

Then, on January 22, 1973, the U.S. Supreme Court, in the preeminent act of judicial supremacy, struck down the anti-abortion laws of all states. As Justice Byron White wrote in dissent, *Roe v. Wade* was "an exercise of raw judicial power ... I find nothing in the language or history of the Constitution to support the Court's judgment." The only Republican justice who dissented was William Rehnquist.

A recent book called *Abuse of Discretion* by Clarke Forsythe spells out the judicial history of *Roe v. Wade*, describing its dishonesty and failure to follow proper judicial procedure and the Court's own precedents. Forsythe's book is based on a close review of the papers of eight of the nine justices who voted in *Roe v. Wade* or *Doe v. Bolton*. The justices originally agreed to hear those two cases only to decide the question of federal versus state jurisdiction.

But a Court crisis erupted in 1971 when two justices, Hugo Black and John Harlan, abruptly retired due to ill health. Reducing the number of justices to seven empowered a temporary majority of four Justices to use those two cases to sweep away all state abortion laws and declare a right to abortion.

Those two cases had no evidentiary record about abortion. There was no trial, no evidence, no expert witness, no record of expert testimony, and no medical data about abortion, its risks or its consequences. None of the statements of sociology, medicine or history used in the *Roe* decision were derived from evidence subjected to the adversary process.

The majority seized upon the claim in a Planned Parenthood brief that a first-trimester abortion is safer than childbirth. That unproved statement significantly influenced

4

the justices to prohibit health and safety regulations in the first trimester, and to add a "health" exception after viability for any reason related to the woman's emotional "well-being."

During the next four decades, hard-fought battles about abortion were waged in Congress, state legislatures, and candidates' campaigns for public office. Various federal and state laws have made obtaining an abortion more difficult than at any time since the 1970s. Pro-life activists successfully lobbied for regulations that limit access, require waiting periods, require ultrasounds, impose safety regulations on clinics, and require minors to get a parent's permission. Fewer doctors are willing to perform abortions, and fewer abortion clinics are open for business.

Gallup polls report that support for abortion rights is fading, particularly among young Americans. More people now identify themselves as pro-life than pro-choice.

In 2014, a federal court upheld a Texas law that prohibits abortion unless the abortionist has hospital privileges within thirty miles. The purpose is so the abortionist can remain available to handle medical complications, instead of letting emergency room costs fall on the taxpayers. Nineteen abortion clinics immediately closed in Texas because of this law. This is the most effective law that states can pass to reduce abortions, and it has been imitated in other states.

The feminists consider abortion the fundamental, irreducible first commandment of feminism. It is usually shrouded in words such as choice, or reproductive freedom, or privacy, or even equal rights, but to feminists, abortion is much more than that. It is the keystone of feminist power over men. As Gloria Steinem opined, the "right of reproductive freedom … attacks the very foundation of patriarchy."

Supreme Court justices Kennedy, O'Connor, and Souter, in *Planned Parenthood v. Casey*, explained the centrality of abortion to feminist ideology. They wrote that, "the ability of women to participate equally in the economic and social life of the Nation has been facilitated by their ability to control their reproductive lives."

The abortion dogma has always had a strong anti-male element. Feminists persuaded the Supreme Court to rule not only that the father has no say as to whether his own baby is killed, but even that the woman has a right *not* to tell her husband that his baby is being killed.

Abortion is the litmus test of whether or not you are feminist. Feminists have even made support of abortion the test of whether a political candidate is waging a "war on women."

When the Supreme Court legalized abortion in *Roe v. Wade* in 1973, many people said the Supreme Court has spoken and *that* ends the debate. But *Roe v. Wade* did not end the controversy; it was the beginning of a long legal and political battle. The American people are not willing for unelected judges to rule our nation.

1976

Starting Republicans on a New Road

Gerald Ford became President in August 1974. He was the only person who ever became President without ever having been nominated for President or Vice President by a Party's National Convention or elected President or Vice President by the voters. Ford was a beneficiary of the 25th Amendment to the U.S. Constitution ratified in 1967. President Nixon was forced to resign after Vice President Spiro Agnew resigned, so the 25th Amendment elevated the unelected Vice President Gerald Ford to the office of President.

First Lady Betty Ford wasted no time in lining up with the feminist movement, declaring *Roe v. Wade* a "great, great decision." When she appeared on CBS 60 Minutes in August 1975, she announced her support of legalized abortion, suggested that premarital sex might cut down on the divorce rate, and said she would not criticize her daughter if she

8

entered into an extramarital affair. Most Republicans pretended not to notice her extremist remarks.

Betty Ford was in line with Republican Party officialdom. Republican National Committee Chair Mary Louise Smith supported abortion rights, and New York Governor Nelson Rockefeller took a leading role in the fight for abortion rights in New York.

The first Republican National Convention after *Roe v. Wade* was in 1976 in Kansas City, Missouri. That year, I served on a subcommittee of the Platform Committee. I offered a motion to include a plank to "protest the Supreme Court's intrusion into the family structure" and to pledge "to seek enactment of a constitutional amendment to restore protection of the right to life for unborn children." The subcommittee approved that language by a vote of thirteen to one, and it was easily approved by the full Platform Committee and then by the National Convention.

At this National Convention, most conservatives were hoping to nominate Ronald Reagan on this, his second try for the nomination. However, the 1976 Convention nominated

Gerald Ford over Ronald Reagan by the narrow vote of 1,187 to 1,070.

U.S. Senator Jesse Helms decided that the 1976 Platform was the place to stand and fight for conservative principles that had eroded under President Gerald Ford, who took advice on most important decisions from Henry Kissinger. It was a tremendous victory for conservatives when the 1976 Convention adopted Jesse Helms' Platform, which repudiated the Nixon-Ford-Kissinger policies about nuclear testing and about accommodation and detente with the Soviet Union.

It was also significant that the 1976 Republican Convention was the first national Convention when the emerging pro-family movement raised its voice in national politics, daring to challenge the U.S. Supreme Court on *Roe v. Wade*.

At the very end of the Convention, President Ford spontaneously turned the microphone over to Reagan, who then delivered one of the most dramatic speeches in all convention history. Speaking extemporaneously for less than five minutes, Reagan reminded his delegates of their accomplishment. "Our Platform is a banner of bold unmistakable colors with no pastel shades," he said. One of those bold unmistakable colors was the first adoption of a Republican Party pledge to "restore protection of the right to life for unborn children."

Some people were hoping that the Democratic Party would also take an anti-abortion position, and a pro-life Democrat, Ellen McCormack of New York, ran for the Democratic nomination for President. She was on the ballot in 18 states and raised enough money to qualify for federal matching funds and Secret Service protection. Her name was placed in nomination at the 1976 Democratic National Convention, but she received only 22 votes. After Mrs. McCormack's valiant effort, the Democratic Party became increasingly inhospitable to pro-life candidates.

1980

Pro-Life Republicans Make Waves

At the 1980 Republican National Convention in Detroit, Michigan, conservative Republicans expected to nominate Ronald Reagan, who had failed to win the nomination so narrowly four years earlier. By the time the Convention convened, it had become clear that (despite the opposition of the kingmakers) Reagan had enough Delegates to be nominated for President. So the media decided to make the big Convention news my fight to remove support of the Equal Rights Amendment (ERA) from the Republican Platform, where it had been resting without controversy for decades.

We didn't realize it until years later, but a major reason why the feminists were so eager to get the Republican Party platform to eliminate support for ERA was that the feminists believed (and later argued in court) that, if ERA put "sex" in the U.S. Constitution, that would force the government to use federal and state taxpayer funds to pay for abortions.

Endorsement of ERA had been a line in the Republican Platform since 1940, and nobody paid much attention to it. However, when the feminists made it a big issue in 1980 and lined up VIPs such as Helen Milliken, wife of the Governor of Michigan; Margaret Heckler, U.S. Congresswoman from Massachusetts; and Mary Dent Crisp, the Republican Party co-chairman, to picket in the streets in favor of ERA, it became necessary for those against ERA to engage in the fight.

We wanted ERA out of the Platform especially because, since Reagan publicly opposed ERA, Platform endorsement of ERA would be an embarrassment to him. The media made the ERA issue a huge media controversy. Later on, when I reviewed the ten years of network TV coverage of the Equal Rights Amendment, 1972 to 1982, I found that 50 percent of the television network minutes devoted to ERA pertained to the 1980 Republican Convention in Detroit.

The media were shocked when the Human Resources Subcommittee, chaired by then-Representative Trent Lott of Mississippi, voted eleven to four for a Women's Rights section

13

that excluded ERA. The media went into cardiac arrest when the full Platform Committee approved the subcommittee's action by a vote of ninety to nine. The media set up a debate between me and Michigan Governor William Milliken on the Today Show, but when the day came, Milliken chickened out and sent Congresswoman Margaret Heckler in his place.

At every Republican Convention, members of the Platform Committee were entertained with a beautiful buffet supper on Sunday evening before the meetings started on Monday. I was not on the Platform Committee in 1980, so I wasn't invited, but I arranged to attend the party on Senator Jesse Helms' arm, so nobody stopped me. Some of our best Eagle advocates were also able to attend the supper party: Najla Lataif, Tottie Ellis, and Shirley Curry. They lobbied the Platform Committee very effectively! The 1980 Platform reaffirmed "support of a constitutional amendment to restore protection of the right to life for unborn children," and added, "We also support the Congressional efforts to restrict the use of taxpayers' dollars for abortion." The feminists' effort to weaken this anti-abortion language failed in the Platform Committee, seventy-five to eighteen.

14

Of course, all Republican National Convention procedures, including voting on the Platform and on all its sections (especially controversial ones), had to go through the relevant subcommittee, and then the full Platform Committee, and finally win approval by the full Convention of some two thousand Delegates. Nearly every change in the Platform had to run the gauntlet of articulate speakers who expressed passionate opinions.

After the subcommittee spent a long afternoon debating and finally agreeing on the language of the section of the Platform about abortion, I realized we would soon be adjourning for dinner, and there would be an unplanned evening when the powers-that-be could attempt to badger, threaten, persuade, or intimidate some subcommittee members (who often were new to the political process) to change their votes. About 6:00 p.m., facing many hours between then and the scheduled meeting of the full Platform Committee at 9:00 a.m. the next morning, I rushed out into the hall and ran into Jimmy Lyons, a wealthy Republican from Houston. I said, "Jimmy, don't you belong to some club in Houston with privileges here in Detroit where we can take this important Subcommittee to dinner?" He replied, "I don't know, but I'll find out."

Jimmy disappeared into a phone booth (this was the pre-cell-phone era when we used phone booths). About ten minutes later, Jimmy came back and said, "I've got you all set up at the Detroit Athletic Club." Of course the dozen members of the subcommittee accepted this gracious invitation, and the party didn't break up until nearly midnight. Several members of the Subcommittee were articulate advocates of our pro-life mission and the flaky members lacked the nerve and the facts to challenge them.

I learned later that the chairman of the Platform Committee, U.S. Senator John Tower of Texas, who was not pro-life, had spent the entire evening trying to call all our Subcommittee members but couldn't reach a single one.

The full Platform Committee convened on schedule at 9:00 a.m. the next morning and approved all our Subcommittee's language.

After those votes were recorded, the co-chairman of the Republican Party, Mary Dent Crisp, who opposed the pro-life plank, went out to meet the press and shed real tears before the television cameras. She then left the Republican Party to support John Anderson as a Third Party candidate, trying to defeat Ronald Reagan. Anderson received only seven percent of the popular vote.

The pro-abortion feminists suffered such a shellacking in Detroit about ERA, they didn't have any energy left to fight the pro-lifers for the votes of the full Convention. We had no difficulty in keeping our pro-life plank in the Platform.

Reagan's election as President in 1980 profoundly changed politics in America. Reagan ended the Nixon-Ford-Kissinger era of detente. Reagan mainstreamed conservatism based on middle-American fiscal and family values. Reagan's vision of conservatism consisted of four elements: limited government with lower taxes; personal responsibility that rejects taxpayer handouts; military superiority to protect American independence; and respect for life and family values.

Each of those four elements has a large constituency and attracted many pro-family Democrats and independents to vote Republican. Reagan gave Americans a true choice, not an echo of all the previous presidential campaigns. In his First Inaugural Address, Reagan proclaimed, "Government is not the solution to our problem; government is the problem."

1984

Locking Pro-Life Into the Platform

The Republican National Convention in 1984 in Dallas was the most successful and enjoyable of all Republican Conventions in the 20th century.

Members of the National Republican Platform Committee are elected by the members of each state's delegation, and the elections are gender specific. One man and one woman are elected to the Platform Committee from each state.

Congressman Henry Hyde and I were the two Delegates elected to the Platform Committee from Illinois, and we led the Committee in adopting this strong and beautiful language:

"The unborn child has a fundamental, individual right to life which cannot be infringed. We therefore reaffirm our support for a human life amendment to the Constitution, and we endorse legislation to make clear that the Fourteenth Amendment's protections apply to unborn children. We oppose the use of public revenues for abortion and will eliminate funding for organizations which advocate or support abortion. … We reaffirm our support for the appointment of judges at all levels of the judiciary who respect traditional family values and the sanctity of innocent human life."

Representative Trent Lott was the chairman of the 1984 national Platform Committee. The pro-life plank wasn't particularly controversial except for a couple of tantrums staged for the media by Senator Lowell Weicker and Representative Nancy Johnson, both from Connecticut. On a voice vote, the full Convention adopted the Platform including our strong pro-life section.

Eagle Forum members have sponsored a party at every Republican National Convention starting in 1964. Our event during the 1984 Convention was a memorable fashion show. Every prominent Republican lady walked in that fashion show, led by Mrs. Jesse Helms and Mrs. Jack Kemp.

Ronald Reagan won reelection in November 1984. He

and the Platform offered voters a clear-cut choice on the issues that matter to Americans: pro-life; national defense; military superiority; fiscal limitation; and pro-family policies.

Instead of Kissinger-style pessimism and defeatism, Reagan offered "morning in America." The 27 million conservatives who voted for Barry Goldwater in 1964 increased their numbers to 54 million in 1984.

1988

Let the Good Times Roll

The 1988 Republican National Convention was scheduled to take place in New Orleans, and Republicans were ready to "let the good times roll." A few Delegates toyed with nominating Jack Kemp or Phil Gramm for President, but George H.W. Bush had flawlessly played the role of second fiddle to Ronald Reagan for eight years (as though he had been singing George Gershwin's "Bidin' My Time") so Bush was easily nominated.

The Family and Community Subcommittee approved the Platform with the same pro-life language that was in the 1984 Platform by a vote of eleven to three, and the full Convention adopted the Platform by a unanimous voice vote.

The Reagan coalition of fiscal and social conservatives loyally stuck together. With Peggy Noonan writing his speeches, George H.W. Bush sounded like Ronald Reagan and

voters assumed Bush would continue Reagan's agenda.
Indeed, voters almost looked upon Bush's election in 1988 as
voting for Ronald Reagan's "third term."

George Bush had the good fortune to draw
Massachusetts' Michael Dukakis as his opponent. While most
politicians were trying to avoid the label of liberal, Dukakis
proudly announced himself "a liberal Democrat" and "a card-
carrying member" of the American Civil Liberties Union.
Dukakis gave us liberalism in one package – a synthesis of
Walter Mondale on taxes, Ted Kennedy and Tip O'Neill on
spending, Geraldine Ferraro on abortion, and George
McGovern on foreign policy.

Bush offered the voters a choice, not an echo on
patriotic, economic, social and pro-life issues, and voters found
it easy to make him the 1988 winner. We successfully kept the
Republican pro-life commitment in the Party's Platform with
the strong 1984 language.

After George H.W. Bush became President, however,
he abandoned many policies of his patron, Ronald Reagan, and
returned to the big-government and globalist policies of his

wealthy friends. Almost the only conservative thing Bush did while President was his nomination of Clarence Thomas to the U.S. Supreme Court. That was, indeed, a great thing for America. Thomas has served as an outstanding constitutionalist and pro-life Justice.

1992

The Year of the Red Cowboy Hats

Trouble started for pro-lifers in 1990. The pro-abortionists began a major campaign to try to scratch pro-life out of the Republican Party and its Platform. A GOP fundraiser, Ann Stone, announced that she had reinvigorated a Planned Parenthood group called "Republicans for Choice" and intended to raise three million dollars to take the pro-life plank out of the Republican Platform.

Almost simultaneously, Mary Dent Crisp, who had been absent politically since her announced support of third-party candidate John Anderson in 1980, started another organization with the same goal. That was very heavy artillery because, of course, they had the media on their side plus many big donors. Conventional wisdom predicted that, at the next Convention in 1992 in Houston, the pro-life plank would become history.

With easy access to the media, Crisp and Stone launched well-publicized threats to remove the pro-life plank from the Republican Platform. They played their trump card in announcing that First Lady Barbara Bush wanted the pro-life plank deleted. However, members of the Platform Committee had worked hard to be elected, so they had minds of their own and remained staunchly pro-life.

The Platform Committee scheduled a special public hearing in Salt Lake City for May 16. When Delegates arrived in Salt Lake City, they were greeted with many billboards and signs reading "Pro Choice." Nicholas Graham, the spokesman for the National Republican Coalition for Choice, announced, "We are going to be a very loud, very annoying voice from here straight through to Houston." The *New York Times* reported that the pro-abortion faction appeared "willing to cause political discomfort for President Bush by waging a public campaign."

At the time that pro-abortion groups made their provocative announcements, three of our best Eagle Forum leaders happened to be in Chicago attending a meeting: Colleen Parro, who was our key Eagle working with me and

General Daniel Graham of High Frontier to support President Reagan in the building of a strong U.S. anti-missile defense; Kathleen Sullivan, president of Illinois Eagle Forum; and Penny Pullen, an Illinois State Representative who was the pro-life leader in the Illinois Legislature.

When they heard the news about the new pro-abortion campaign, they immediately went to a phone booth, called me and said, "We have to do something!" "Well," I replied, "America has many good pro-life organizations. They can take care of this problem."

I then phoned all the national pro-life organizations and asked them if they were going to take on the project of stopping those prominent women, who had the support of money and the media, from taking the pro-life plank out of the Republican Platform. They all said "No" because they wanted to be non-partisan and not ally their organizations with any political party.

Well, I've never been nonpartisan. I believe the Republican Party must be the vehicle to achieve the good things we want for our country, which is why I've run for and been elected a Republican Convention Delegate so many times. The bottom line was, "Phyllis, you have to do it." So Colleen Parro and I started Republican National Coalition for Life.

To launch our new organization, I planned a special luncheon at a top-scale hotel in Washington, DC with several people we wanted to join our effort – Beverly LaHaye, Gary Bauer, and a couple of major donors I was hoping would help finance our new project. I alerted the hotel that one of those important donors, Pat Rooney, was a vegetarian, so he should be given a nice vegetarian plate. In the middle of my impassioned speech asking for support for our new organization, the waiter walked in with a big plate that had nothing on it except twelve sprigs of broccoli arranged like a clock and a lonely carrot in the middle. That threw my speech off course, but we survived the interruption and continued to spell out our goals.

It wasn't hard to anticipate that we would face a big fight about abortion at the Republican National Convention in Houston in 1992 when George H.W. Bush would be up for re-nomination. He was declining in the polls and squishing on pro-life, and the pro-abortion crowd thought they had a good opportunity to change course for Republicans.

Colleen Parro did a fantastic job of identifying pro-life and Eagle Forum leaders in a majority of states, urging them to become Delegates to their state Republican Convention. She educated them on how to run for and get elected as Delegates to the Republican National Convention and how to run for and win a seat on the national Platform Committee. RNC for Life booths cropped up at state conventions across the country, equipped with red, white and blue banners, bumper stickers, and RNC/Life buttons. By the time we arrived at the 1992 Convention, we had identified our pro-life Delegates and believed that, if a floor fight occurred, we would win.

It's not easy to be elected a Delegate to a Republican Convention. I had to be elected at a caucus of my Township, and then elected again in a caucus of my State Legislative District, and then elected again in my Congressional District caucus and elected again by the state Republican convention. Then, to be on the Platform Committee I had to be elected by a vote at the first caucus of all the state's elected national Convention Delegates. This takes planning and making friends with people active in the Republican Party. (We now need hundreds of pro-lifers to make similar plans to be elected to the 2016 Convention, which is scheduled to be in Cleveland, Ohio.)

In 1992, we set a goal to get all Republican public officials to sign a pledge to support the pro-life plank in the Platform, and we did get nearly all the prominent Republicans to sign our pledge, from Newt Gingrich on down to local officeholders. We packaged the tens of thousands of signed pledges in a separate decorated and labeled box for each of the fifty states.

To make a splash at the Republican Convention in Houston, we decided that our insignia would be red cowboy hats. We bought three thousand large red cowboy hats (guaranteed to be made in the U.S., not in China) to be delivered to our Eagle Susan Feldtman's living room in Houston. We passed them out to Convention Delegates and they absolutely loved them. Nobody rejected wearing a red hat.

We were very tolerant and let Delegates wear our hats even if they were not really pro-life because the hats looked so impressive on television. It soon looked like everybody was wearing a pro-life hat. We staged a news conference with many attractive young Republicans wearing the hats and admiring the fifty state boxes filled with pro-life pledges. At the appropriate time in the news conference, we rolled out a tremendous stream of signatures from Republican officeholders.

We were receiving about as much media as the pro-abortion crowd. Our new Republican National Coalition for Life became the sponsor of our event, and our sellout crowd filled the Houston Civic Center. Rush Limbaugh was our star speaker, backed up by other dignitaries such as Jerry Falwell and Vice President Dan Quayle.

The Subcommittee on Individual Rights, Good Homes and Safe Streets, chaired by Mary Potter Summa of North Carolina, conducted a dignified session with full debate, after which the vote was seventeen to three to retain the pro-life language of the 1984 Platform. The full Platform Committee then approved the pro-life Platform commitment by a vote of eighty-four to ten. On the first day of the Convention, the full Convention adopted the Platform by a unanimous voice vote.

After George H.W. Bush lost the 1992 election to Bill Clinton, the media orchestrated a campaign to blame his defeat on the pro-lifers and those who had talked about the social issues, such as Pat Buchanan and Dan and Marilyn Quayle. However, the TV networks' own polls conducted right after the Convention reported that the Buchanan and Quayle speeches actually gave George Bush a big boost with the voters.

1996

Don't Change a Comma

At the 1996 Republican National Convention in San Diego, our goal was to retain the pro-life plank exactly as we had written it in 1984 in Dallas.

We adopted the slogan that we can't change a word "or a comma" because, if we did, that would give the media the opportunity to report that we had softened our solid pro-life position. Ann Stone was still hanging around.

As we geared up for the election, the media and the kingmakers launched a campaign to persuade Republican Delegates to nominate Colin Powell for President. But because he was a neophyte in political semantics, Powell made so many bloopers that his campaign rapidly ran aground. The worst was proclaiming himself "pro-choice."

So the kingmakers settled on Bob Dole even though

they were never really comfortable with him or his political tactics. Even the *New York Times* expressed bewilderment that Dole failed to campaign on any social issues or attack Clinton's veto of the very popular ban on partial-birth abortion. A *Times* front page headline taunted him: "Dole Silent on Social Issues."

Colleen Parro was in constant touch with pro-life Republicans, encouraging them to elect the right people as National Delegates and especially to the Platform Committee. She trained them for political battles because we understood that our battle was political as well as moral and ideological.

Colleen Parro and I went to San Diego weeks before the Convention to select a headquarters and a place for our usual pro-life party. That's always a challenge because, months before a Convention meets, the Republican bigwigs lock up all the venues, all the hotels, and all the places where you can have parties, so that the Party controls everything in the city.

However, we were able to find a small hotel right across from the Convention Hall that was in bankruptcy, so it hadn't made it onto the Party's approved list. That's where we set up our headquarters. Pat Buchanan (for whom I was a delegate) and Gary Bauer, Chairman of the Family Research Council, were able to locate their headquarters there, too. At this San Diego Convention, we used white cowboy hats as our RNC for Life insignia.

Meanwhile, the pro-abortion Republicans were working very hard to water down the pro-life plank if they couldn't eliminate it altogether. When Arlen Specter announced his candidacy for President in 1996, he said his number-one goal was to get rid of the pro-life plank in the Republican Platform. Pete Wilson had just been reelected Governor of California with a larger majority than Reagan ever received, and he announced he was running for President on the number-one goal of taking pro-life language out of the Republican Platform. Again, we had very heavy ammunition aimed against our pro-life cause.

New Jersey Governor Christine Todd Whitman, who was widely predicted by TV pundits (such as John McLaughlin) as sure to get the Republican Vice-Presidential nomination in 1996 regardless of who was nominated for President, told a news conference on July 11, "The anti-abortion plank in the Republican Party Platform should be knocked out entirely. I don't even want to mess with modification, I just want it out of there."

Of course, pro-lifers wanted to have a "fun" party, so what's the biggest thing in San Diego? Shamu the whale, of course. I went to Sea World and made a deal for our party (with the whale) and signed the contract just thirty minutes before Republican officials discovered that venue. Our "Whale of a Party" at Sea World was another big success, attracting 1,300 people. Our star attraction, Shamu, performed on schedule.

Meanwhile, the kingmakers' candidate, Bob Dole, was steadily moving toward his nomination for President. That year, the chairman of the Platform Committee happened to be Congressman Henry Hyde, a lifelong personal and political friend of mine in Illinois and a nationally respected and articulate pro-life leader. That should have made our pro-life mission easy.

But there was one big problem: Henry Hyde was also a long-time buddy-buddy of Bob Dole and didn't want anything to harm Dole's election prospects as President.

Before every Republican Convention, we in RNC for Life would identify our true believers on the Platform Committee, and have a dinner for them ahead of time to plan our strategy. In San Diego, to make sure nobody could spy on us, we planned our caucus in a restaurant where we had to climb two steep flights of stairs (no elevator available).

Bob Dole was not easy to deal with. He wanted to get rid of the pro-life Platform plank because we were still in the era when Republican strategists were advising all candidates not to talk about social issues, especially about abortion. Dole wanted to purge the pro-life language altogether, but his "Plan B" was to add additional language to the Platform about promoting "tolerance." Our pro-lifers didn't want to say we're tolerant of abortion; that was not on our agenda.

During that summer of 1996, Dole shot himself in the foot several times. He had promised his pro-abortion supporters that he would either get rid of, or water down, the Party's pro-life plank. On June 10, Dole stated on CNN that a "tolerance" statement is "going to be in the abortion plank," adding, "I make that decision and it's not negotiable."

Dole apparently didn't know that the Presidential nominee could no longer dictate the Platform as Richard Nixon and Nelson Rockefeller dictated it in 1960. The Republican Platform Committee consists of one man and one woman elected from each state by all the members of their state's delegation. Republicans work hard to be elected, first as a delegate and then to the Platform Committee, so they take their responsibilities seriously.

I invited Platform Committee chairman Henry Hyde to attend our dinner at that little upstairs restaurant. I cordially introduced him, and then called on each Platform Delegate around the table to have a say about the pro-life plank. After we got halfway around the table, Congressman Hyde stood up and walked out. He realized that we were an "immovable rock," not willing to weaken our pro-life Platform commitment by any "tolerance" language.

Meanwhile, we were also working with Bob Dole's staff, whom Dole was checking with constantly, giving orders, getting information, and stating his demands. Finally, Dole's staff pulled the telephone plug out of the wall so they couldn't hear from him anymore.

The 1996 Platform Committee treated the pro-abortionists courteously and allowed them lengthy time to make their arguments, but the largest number of votes they received was 11 out of 107, a decline from the 16 they had received at the 1992 Convention in Houston. Eleven was not enough even to file a minority report.

Bob Dole then insulted the Delegates by announcing to the press, "I haven't read the platform and I'm not bound by it anyway." Dole's political strategists deleted the life, cultural, and sovereignty issues out of Dole's campaign. He then personally demanded that the following be added to the Party's Platform, and the weary committee included it: "We are the party of the open door ... we welcome into our ranks all those Americans who may hold differing positions." The committee humored Dole by including this, although it was obvious that he didn't believe it himself. Dole's convention managers soon made it crystal clear that the concepts of "open door," "diversity," welcoming "differing positions," "civility," and "mutual respect" applied only to the pro-abortion Rockefeller

Republicans – not to pro-lifers.

Despite the difficulties with Bob Dole, we won our Platform battle again. The Committee wrote a conservative, pro-life document that was unanimously adopted by the full convention on August 12. The key part of the 1996 Republican Platform was approved just as we wrote it in Dallas in 1984, and it did not include any Dole "tolerance" language. The pro-abortion crowd hung around in the halls but didn't have any influence. One of them complained to the press, "We are excluded, unwanted, untolerated, and unhappy."

The media labeled the winners in San Diego the "Fearsome Foursome" consisting of: Ralph Reed, executive director of the Christian Coalition; Bay Buchanan, sister of Pat; Gary Bauer, chairman of the Family Research Council; and me.

2000

Pro-Life Becomes the *Life* of the Party

The next Convention was in 2000 in Philadelphia where, again, we had a fabulous RNC for Life party. Held at the Philadelphia Union League Club, it was another great success. The bitter pro-abortion feminists were picketing outside the Union League Club, but they were ignored. Our signature giveaway in Philadelphia was vests for all pro-life Delegates inscribed with the words, "The *Life* of the Party." That became our slogan; proclaiming that pro-lifers are truly "the *LIFE* of the Party."

The grassroots were so hungry to win back the White House after two terms of Bill Clinton that they were willing to tolerate Bush's deviations from conservative orthodoxy on many issues – but not on the sanctity of life. When the pro-abortion Governor of Pennsylvania, Tom Ridge, was floated as a possible running mate for Bush, pro-lifers quashed that bad idea by telling the *New York Times* that Bush would lose if he

41

chose Ridge.

The 2000 Platform that we adopted was very strong both for life *and* for marriage. It read, "The unborn baby has a fundamental individual right to life" and "We support the traditional definition of marriage as the legal union of one man and one woman."

The pro-abortion minority in the Party staged its usual tantrums to get media coverage, but they were not successful in eliminating either the pro-life plank or the marriage plank in the Platform.

2004

Sticking By Our Principles

The 2004 Republican National Convention was in New York City. Journalists were amazed at the tight control that the Bush Administration tried to exercise over the Platform Committee that year. One journalist commented that the Bush language dumped on the Platform Committee was kept as secret as the Manhattan Project and then handed down from on high like the Ten Commandments. Bush was praised on most of the 98 pages in the platform.

However, by 2004, it had become conventional wisdom that the Establishment had better not try to remove the pro-life language because we were determined to keep the plank just as we wrote it in 1984, word for word. We liked the language we had, and we didn't want it muddied up or watered down. We hosted our New York party at the Tavern on the Green featuring Ann Coulter and other valiant pro-lifers to whom we presented awards.

So Bush went along with the committee's retention of the same pro-life language that had been in the platform since 1984. Respect for the right to life of unborn babies has been official Republican Party doctrine ever since *Roe v. Wade,* and Republicans believe that the pro-life constituency is essential to political victories.

2008

Overcoming Unexpected Problems

By the time we got to St. Paul, Minnesota, the 2008 Convention city, pro-life wasn't a big battle any more. Only a few disgruntled pro-aborts tried to continue the fight. We had established the Republican Party as *the* pro-life Party. It was now difficult for anybody to get a Republican nomination who didn't say he was pro-life. They may not have been as totally pro-life as many of us are, but nearly all Republican candidates now like to say they are pro-life.

RNC for Life had, and still has, a very detailed questionnaire that candidates are required to fill out if they want our endorsement.

Many months before the 2008 National Convention, we had signed up Alaska Governor Sarah Palin to be the featured speaker at our Republican National Coalition for Life

45

Luncheon. She was a rising star and we were confident she would be a big attraction for our pro-life event.

The day before our long-planned big RNC for Life event at the Crowne Plaza Hotel in St. Paul, the managers of the John McCain for President Campaign ordered Sarah Palin to cancel her appearance. After McCain named her as his Vice Presidential running mate, he didn't want her speaking to any event he didn't control.

You can imagine how hard that hit us; it would have absolutely destroyed the beautiful event we had been planning for six months. I worried that I would be expected to refund all the money we had received for tickets to this expensive event.

The good Lord came to our rescue. Suddenly the phone rang, and it was Laura Ingraham. She said, "I just arrived in St. Paul. Can I come to your party tomorrow?"

Welcome, Laura! Substituting for Sarah Palin, Laura Ingraham gave a tremendous speech, and nobody was disappointed.

One other event made that luncheon memorable. As our program started, I was introducing the dignitaries before I presented Laura Ingraham. Suddenly a troublemaker from a leftwing outfit called "Code Pink" rushed up on the stage carrying an obnoxious sign and tried to wrestle the microphone away from me. I fought her off until two Texans wearing cowboy hats came on the stage to rescue me. The audience loved the fight.

Our RNC for Life Event in St. Paul turned out to be one of our most memorable and successful.

2012

America Is Becoming Pro-Life

P ro-lifers are not only winning in the Republican Party; we're winning nationwide. Public opinion polls show that the majority of Americans now say they're pro-life. The whole country is coming our way and I am particularly cheered when I talk to young people. National public opinion polls confirm that young people are more pro-life than older people. It's very important that we keep on nominating candidates who are pro-life, and will vote pro-life and stick with us on the issues that are important to pro-life, such as the confirmation of judges.

It's been a tremendous fight, and RNC for Life together with Eagle Forum has led the battle. We have made it essential for Republican candidates to be pro-life. We are winning through the political process: nominating and electing candidates to public office; electing Delegates to the Republican National Conventions; and persuading Delegates on the Platform Committee to vote pro-life.

On January 22, 2014, the members of the entire Republican National Committee made history when they gathered in the lobby of the Renaissance Hotel in downtown Washington, DC. Buttoning up their coats on a winter day, each was handed a red baseball cap with RNC emblazoned across the front. This participation in the March for Life was arranged by the newly elected president of Eagle Forum, Ed Martin, and facilitated by Republican National Chairman Reince Priebus, who adjusted the agenda of a regular national RNC meeting to accommodate members' participation in the March for Life.

After a short bus ride across downtown to the Mall, they joined tens of thousands of Americans in the 41st annual March for Life, making a dramatic statement of how genuinely pro-life the Republican Party has become. Gone are the days when Republicans remained silent after an obviously wrong, unconstitutional and immoral decision by supremacist judges.

However, we are not ready to fold our tents and claim the battle for pro-life is over. The anti-life kingmakers and the high-paid strategists who advise our candidates, are still telling their clients and the recipients of their big campaign donations to avoid the moral and social issues.

The pro-life battle won't be over until we quash the unconstitutional push for judicial supremacy. It is clearly an un-American notion that one judge, or even a 5-to-4 majority of judges (none of whom is elected by the voters) can rewrite portions of our Constitution or declare that a human being (such as a baby in the womb) is the property of somebody else and can be killed by its alleged owner.

Our Constitution created a government of three co-equal branches, and certainly did not give the judicial branch the right to overrule the other branches.

In other words, pro-lifers can't celebrate victory until we expunge *Roe v. Wade* and *Doe v. Bolton* from having any constitutional authority or significance as a legal precedent.

We must assume that the pro-abortion faction, which has always been able to raise big bucks and prop up important people to speak for their cause, won't go away, but will be carrying on their mischief again at the 2016 Republican National Convention in Cleveland, Ohio. Pro-lifers must be in Cleveland in force to protect the tremendous gains we have made. This requires engaging in rough-and-tumble party politics in order to elect Delegates to that Convention who will retain the Republican position as the pro-life party.

Rejecting Judicial Supremacy

The Republican Party was born on the principle that no human being should be considered the property of another. That is our heritage as Republicans.

The most famous political debates in American history were the Lincoln-Douglas Debates of 1858. During those seven debates up and down the State of Illinois, Abraham Lincoln enunciated the position of the then-new Republican Party that slavery was "a moral, a social and a political wrong," and that he "looks forward to a time when slavery shall be abolished everywhere."

The Democratic candidate, Stephen A. Douglas, argued that the Supreme Court's ruling in *Dred Scott v. Sandford* had settled the slavery question once and for all. Saying, "I choose to abide by the decisions of the Supreme Court as they are pronounced," Douglas argued that everyone was bound to accept the Court's decision that the U.S. Constitution protects an individual property right in slaves throughout the United States and its Western territories.

Abraham Lincoln did not dispute the authority of the Supreme Court to decide a particular case, but he forthrightly proclaimed, "We do not propose to be bound by it as a political rule. We propose to have it reversed if we can, and a new judicial rule established upon this subject."

Lincoln thus rejected *judicial supremacy*, the notion that major constitutional decisions can be made by what he called "that eminent tribunal" instead of by "we the people."

In Quincy, Illinois, Lincoln argued that we should "deal with [slavery] as with any other wrong, insofar as we can prevent its growing any larger, and deal with it that, in the run of time, there may be some promise of an end to it. We have a due regard to the actual presence of it amongst us and the difficulties of getting rid of it in any satisfactory way ... [but] we oppose it as an evil."

As authority for saying that slavery was "wrong," Lincoln cited our nation's founding document, the Declaration of Independence, which asserts as a "self-evident" truth that each of us is "endowed by their Creator" with unalienable rights of life and liberty, and that government is instituted for the purpose of securing those rights.

"The real issue in this controversy," Lincoln said in the Alton, Illinois, debate, is that the Republican Party "looks upon the institution of slavery as a wrong" and the Democratic Party "does not look upon it as a wrong." Lincoln proclaimed that the slavery issue represented "the eternal struggle between these two principles – right and wrong."

In reporting the Lincoln-Douglas debates, the biased press of the 1850s called Lincoln "a dead dog" walking to his "political grave," and reported Stephen Douglas' arguments as "logical" and "powerful." Lincoln lost that Senatorial election to Douglas. But two years later, in a rematch against Senator Douglas, Abraham Lincoln was elected our first Republican President – and the verdict of history is on Lincoln's side.

Abortion is the right-or-wrong issue of our time. We should parallel the words of Abraham Lincoln today and say, "The Republican Party looks upon abortion as a wrong, and the

Democratic Party does not look upon it as a wrong." That's the crucial difference between the two parties.

Republicans must not adopt the Stephen Douglas position that a wrong Supreme Court decision is infallible and irrevocable. We must repudiate the 1973 Supreme Court decision in *Roe v. Wade*, which legalized the deliberate killing of unborn babies.

The Declaration of Independence does not mention abortion, but you will search in vain for a single affirmation that the Creator-endowed right to life was to be withheld from a baby until the moment of birth. Every new advance in science, especially the DNA and the ultra-sound photographs of babies in the womb, confirms that the unique, individual identity of each of us is present, human, alive and growing even before the mother realizes she is pregnant.

The Republican Party's position as the pro-life party was arrived at through the democratic process and maintained consistently through ten Republican National Conventions and Platforms in 1976, 1980, 1984, 1988, 1992, 1996, 2000, 2004,

2008, and 2012. A Party Platform is a standard, a banner to raise on high, to proclaim our general principles and display our convictions. It is not legislation. Our Platform is strong on strategic principle, while leaving details and tactics to the legislative process.

The Republican Party was founded on the principle that no human being should be considered the property of another, and on a repudiation of a U.S. Supreme Court which had ruled otherwise.

We reject rule by supremacist judges who espouse heretical notions that our U.S. Constitution is a "living" or "evolving" document that Supreme Court justices can amend or rewrite. We call for a return to government by "we the people" expressing their will through our three co-equal branches of government. When supremacist judges presume to rewrite portions of our law, most especially if it is a law that we have had for millennia such as our law defining marriage, it's time for the American people to speak up and say "No" just as Abe Lincoln did when supremacist judges ruled that blacks could be considered another man's "property."

On March 8, 2004 President Bush delivered this challenge: "We will not stand for judges who undermine democracy by legislating from the bench and try to remake the culture of America by court order." Every presidential candidate should be asked to repeat that pledge.

What kind of a country do we want America to be? Do we want a country where "we the people" are sovereign, where we are governed by legislators we elect, where we can continue to raise our children in a land where the government respects our religious, cultural and family rights? Or will we allow ourselves to be ruled by an unelected cadre of judges?

All those who love liberty must oppose judicial supremacy and its advocates. In the words of the Declaration of Independence, we must disavow these "usurpations."

Likewise in the marriage case, we reject the notion that an unelected judge can rewrite our definition of marriage that has been a part of our law and culture for millennia. All Americans must use every tool in the political process to reject judicial supremacy and return to government by "we the people."

Afterword

Over the past few years I have given hundreds of talks on college campuses and spoken to thousands of young people. I have learned that an important lesson that I can give these young students for life is this: victory is possible and that the hard fought battles are the ones worth fighting.

Phyllis Schlafly is a hero of mine – and of many people for many reasons. She is a clear and persuasive writer of more than 25 books and thousands of columns. She is a classy woman who delivers powerful speeches. I have been impressed by her career of service, her ability to build a national organization, and her joy in fighting the good fight.

What you have just read is the heretofore untold story of how a band of pro-lifers went about changing the course of American history by changing the Republican Party. After the 1973 Roe v. Wade abortion decision, Phyllis and those early pro-lifers refused to accept the conventional wisdom – offered by national Republican leaders as well as media pundits – that the "Supreme Court has spoken, it's the law of the land, and folks need to get over it and move on."

Phyllis rejected this advice and built a pro-life army who set about making the Republican Party pro-life. They started with a pro-life plank in the Republican platform. Phyllis started RNC for Life, a pro-life organization focused on supporting pro-life Republicans. Over the decades, Phyllis and her army defended the pro-life plank and grew the size and strength of their membership. Today, there is no national Republican candidate who dares be anything other than pro-life!

If you care about winning, this book helps us understand how to win. If you care about inspiring others, this book shows us how to emulate Phyllis. More than anything if you care to know why America is great and why her people will always step up for the true and good fights, this book clearly declares what is behind a core value of the Republican Party today, and of our nation.

After reading this book, I hope that you can now see clearly why Phyllis Schlafly is a great American hero.

Kristan Hawkins
President, Students for Life of America

Appendix A
Pro-Life References
in Republican Platforms

1976

The American Family

Families must continue to be the foundation of our nation.

Families—not government programs—are the best way to make sure our children are properly nurtured, our elderly are cared for, our cultural and spiritual heritages are perpetuated, our laws are observed and our values are preserved.

Because of our concern for family values, we affirm our beliefs, stated elsewhere in this Platform, in many elements that will make our country a more hospitable environment for family life—neighborhood schools; educational systems that include and are responsive to parents' concerns; estate tax changes to establish more realistic exemptions which will minimize disruption of already bereaved families; a position on abortion that values human life; a welfare policy to encourage rather than discourage families to stay together and seek economic independence; a tax system that assists rather than penalizes families with elderly members, children in day care or children in college; economic and employment policies that stop the shrinkage of our dollars and stimulate the creation of jobs so that families can plan for their economic security.

While we support valid medical and biological research efforts which can produce life-saving results, we oppose any research on live fetuses. We are also opposed to any legislation which sanctions ending the life of any patient.

We protest the Supreme Court's intrusion into the family structure through its denial of the parents' obligation and right to guide their minor children. The Republican Party favors a continuance of the public dialogue on abortion and supports the efforts of those who seek enactment of a constitutional amendment to restore protection of the right to life for unborn children.

1980

Abortion

There can be no doubt that the question of abortion, despite the complex nature of its various issues, is ultimately concerned with equality of rights under the law. While we recognize differing views on this question among Americans in general— and in our own Party—we affirm our support of a constitutional amendment to restore protection of the right to life for unborn children. We also support the Congressional efforts to restrict the use of taxpayers' dollars for abortion.

1984

Our Constitutional System

The unborn child has a fundamental individual right to life which cannot be infringed. We therefore reaffirm our support for a human life amendment to the Constitution, and we endorse legislation to make clear that the Fourteenth Amendment's protections apply to unborn children. We oppose the use of public revenues for abortion and will eliminate funding for organizations which advocate or support abortion.

We commend the efforts of those individuals and religious and private organizations that are providing positive alternatives to abortion by meeting the physical, emotional, and financial needs of pregnant women and offering adoption services where needed.

We applaud President Reagan's fine record of judicial appointments, and we reaffirm our support for the appointment of judges at all levels of the judiciary who respect traditional family values and the sanctity of innocent human life.

1988

Constitutional Government and Individual Rights
The unborn child has a fundamental individual right to life which cannot be infringed. We therefore reaffirm our support for a human life amendment to the Constitution, and we endorse legislation to make clear that the Fourteenth Amendment's protections apply to unborn children. We oppose the use of public revenues for abortion and will eliminate funding for organizations which advocate or support abortion. We commend the efforts of those individuals and religious and private organizations that are providing positive alternatives to

abortion by meeting the physical, emotional, and financial needs of pregnant women and offering adoption services where needed.

We applaud President Reagan's fine record of judicial appointments, and we reaffirm our support for the appointment of judges at all levels of the judiciary who respect traditional family values and the sanctity of innocent human life.

Values are the core of good education. A free society needs a moral foundation for its learning. We oppose any programs in public schools which provide birth control or abortion services or referrals. Our "first line of defense" to protect our youth from contracting AIDS and other sexually communicable diseases, from teen pregnancy, and from illegal drug use must be abstinence education.

1992

Individual Rights
The protection of individual rights is the foundation for opportunity and security.

… We believe the unborn child has a fundamental individual right to life which cannot be infringed. We therefore reaffirm our support for a human life amendment to the Constitution, and we endorse legislation to make clear that the Fourteenth Amendment's protections apply to unborn children. We oppose using public revenues for abortion and will not fund organizations which advocate it. We commend those who provide alternatives to abortion by meeting the needs of mothers and offering adoption services. We reaffirm our support for appointment of judges who respect traditional family values and the sanctity of innocent human life.

… Accordingly, we oppose programs in public schools that provide birth control or abortion services or referrals. Instead, we encourage abstinence education programs with proven track records in protecting youth from disease, pregnancy, and drug use.

… Because we uphold the family as the building block of economic progress, we protect its rights in international programs and will continue to withhold funds from organizations involved in abortion.

1996

Principles

… Because institutions like the family are the backbone of a healthy society, we believe government must support the rights of the family; and recognizing within our own ranks different approaches toward our common goal, we reaffirm respect for the sanctity of human life.

The unborn child has a fundamental individual right to life which cannot be infringed. We support a human life amendment to the Constitution and we endorse legislation to make clear that the Fourteenth Amendment's protections apply to unborn children. Our purpose is to have legislative and judicial protection of that right against those who perform abortions. We oppose using public revenues for abortion and will not fund organizations which advocate it. We support the appointment of judges who respect traditional family values and the sanctity of innocent human life.

Our goal is to ensure that women with problem pregnancies have the kind of support, material and otherwise, they need for themselves and for their babies, not to be punitive towards those for whose difficult situation we have only compassion. We oppose abortion, but our pro-life agenda does not include punitive action against women who have an abortion. We salute those who provide alternatives to abortion and offer adoption services. Republicans in Congress took the lead in expanding assistance both for the costs of adoption and for the continuing care of adoptive children with special needs.

Human nature and aspirations are the same everywhere, and everywhere the family is the building block of economic and social progress. We therefore will protect the rights of families in international programs and will not fund organizations involved in abortion.

Abstinence education in the home will lead to less need for birth control services and fewer abortions. We support educational initiatives to promote chastity until marriage as the expected standard of behavior. This education initiative is the best preventive measure to avoid the emotional trauma of sexually-transmitted diseases and teen pregnancies that are serious problems among our young people. While recognizing that something must be done to help children when parental consent or supervision is not possible, we oppose school-based clinics, which provide referrals, counseling, and related services for contraception and abortion.

2000

Upholding the Rights of All

The Supreme Court's recent decision, prohibiting states from banning partial-birth abortions—a procedure denounced by a committee of the American Medical Association and rightly branded as four-fifths infanticide—shocks the conscience of the nation. As a country, we must keep our pledge to the first guarantee of the Declaration of Independence. That is why we say the unborn child has a fundamental individual right to life which cannot be infringed. We support a human life amendment to the Constitution and we endorse legislation to make clear that the Fourteenth Amendment's protections apply to unborn children. Our purpose is to have legislative and judicial protection of that right against those who perform abortions. We oppose using public revenues for abortion and will not fund organizations which advocate it. We support the appointment of judges who respect traditional family values and the sanctity of innocent human life.

Our goal is to ensure that women with problem pregnancies have the kind of support, material and otherwise, they need for themselves and for their babies, not to be punitive towards those for whose difficult situation we have only compassion. We oppose abortion, but our pro-life agenda does not include punitive action against women who have an abortion. We salute those who provide alternatives to abortion and offer adoption services, and we commend congressional Republicans for expanding assistance to adopting families and for removing racial barriers to adoption.

Children At Risk

… We renew our call for replacing "family planning" programs for teens with increased funding for abstinence education, which teaches abstinence until marriage as the responsible and expected standard of behavior.

The United Nations

The United Nations was created to benefit all peoples and nations, not to promote a radical agenda of social engineering. Any effort to address global social problems must be firmly placed into a context of respect for the fundamental social institutions of marriage and family. We reject any treaty or convention that would contradict these values. For that reason, we will protect the rights of families in international programs and will not fund organizations involved in abortion.

2004

International Institutions

Any effort to address global social problems must be firmly placed within a context of respect for the fundamental social institutions of marriage and family. We reject any treaty or convention that would contradict these values. For that reason, we support protecting the rights of families in international programs and oppose funding organizations involved in abortion.

Supporting Judges Who Uphold the Law

In the federal courts, scores of judges with activist backgrounds in the hard-left now have lifetime tenure. Recent events have made it clear that these judges threaten America's dearest institutions and our very way of life. In some states, activist judges are redefining the institution of marriage. While the vast majority of Americans support a ban on partial-birth abortion, this brutal and violent practice will likely continue by judicial fiat. We believe that the self-proclaimed supremacy of these judicial activists is antithetical to the democratic ideals on which our nation was founded.

Promoting Healthy Choices, Including Abstinence

We oppose school-based clinics that provide referrals, counseling, and related services for contraception and abortion.

Promoting a Culture of Life

As a country, we must keep our pledge to the first guarantee of the Declaration of Independence. That is why we say the unborn child has a fundamental individual right to life which cannot be infringed. We support a human life amendment to the Constitution and we endorse legislation to make it clear that the Fourteenth Amendment's protections apply to unborn children. Our purpose is to have legislative and judicial protection of that right against those who perform abortions. We oppose using public revenues for abortion and will not fund organizations which advocate it. We support the appointment of judges who respect traditional family values and the sanctity of innocent human life.

71

2008

Maintaining The Sanctity and Dignity of Human Life

At its core, abortion is a fundamental assault on the sanctity of innocent human life. Women deserve better than abortion. Every effort should be made to work with women considering abortion to enable and empower them to choose life. We salute those who provide them alternatives, including pregnancy care centers.

Securing the Peace - Sovereign American Leadership in International Organizations

... Because the UN has no mandate to promote radical social engineering, any effort to address global social problems must respect the fundamental institutions of marriage and family. We assert the rights of families in all international programs and will not fund organizations involved in abortion. We strongly support the long-held policy of the Republican Party known as the "Mexico City policy," which prohibits federal monies from being given to non-governmental organizations that provide abortions or actively promote abortion as a method of family planning in other countries. We reject any treaty or agreement that would violate those values.

Patient Control and Portability

Because the family is our basic unit of society, we fully support parental rights to consent to medical treatment for their children including mental health treatment, drug treatment, alcohol treatment, and treatment involving pregnancy, contraceptives and abortion.

Principles for Elementary and Secondary Education

We renew our call for replacing "family planning" programs for teens with increased funding for abstinence education, which teaches abstinence until marriage as the responsible and expected standard of behavior. Abstinence from sexual activity is the only protection that is 100 percent effective against out-of-wedlock pregnancies and sexually transmitted diseases, including HIV/AIDS when transmitted sexually. We oppose school-based clinics that provide referrals, counseling, and related services for abortion and contraception. Schools should not ask children to answer offensive or intrusive personal nonacademic questionnaires without parental consent.

2012

The Sanctity and Dignity of Human Life

Faithful to the "self-evident" truths enshrined in the Declaration of Independence, we assert the sanctity of human life and affirm that the unborn child has a fundamental individual right to life which cannot be infringed. We support a human life amendment to the Constitution and endorse legislation to make clear that the Fourteenth Amendment's protections apply to unborn children. We oppose using public revenues to promote or perform abortion or fund organizations which perform or advocate it and will not fund or subsidize health care which includes abortion coverage. We support the appointment of judges who respect traditional family values and the sanctity of innocent human life.

Republican leadership has led the effort to prohibit the barbaric practice of partial-birth abortion and permitted States to extend health care coverage to children before birth. We urge Congress to strengthen the Born Alive Infant Protection Act by enacting appropriate civil and criminal penalties on healthcare providers who fail to provide treatment and care to an infant who survives an abortion, including early induction delivery where the death of the infant is intended. We call for legislation to ban sex-selective abortions—gender discrimination in its most lethal form—and to protect from abortion unborn children who are capable of feeling pain; and we applaud U.S. House Republicans for leading the effort to protect the lives of pain-capable unborn children in the District of Columbia. We call for a ban on the use of body parts from aborted fetuses for research. We support and applaud adult stem cell research to develop lifesaving therapies, and we oppose the killing of embryos for their stem cells. We oppose federal funding of embryonic stem cell research.

We also salute the many States that have passed laws for informed consent, mandatory waiting periods prior to an abortion, and health-protective clinic regulation. We seek to protect young girls from exploitation through a parental consent requirement; and we affirm our moral obligation to assist, rather than penalize, women challenged by an unplanned pregnancy. We salute those who provide them with counseling and adoption alternatives and empower them to choose life, and we take comfort in the tremendous increase in adoptions that has followed Republican legislative initiatives.

Appendix B
Pro-Marriage References
in Republican Platforms

1856

Resolved: That the Constitution confers upon Congress sovereign powers over the Territories of the United States for their government; and that in the exercise of this power, it is both the right and the imperative duty of Congress to prohibit in the Territories those twin relics of barbarism—Polygamy, and Slavery.

1992

We oppose any legislation or law which legally recognizes same-sex marriages and allows such couples to adopt children or provide foster care.

1996

The sole source of equal opportunity for all is equality before the law. Therefore, we oppose discrimination based on sex, race, age, creed, or national origin and will vigorously enforce anti-discrimination statutes. We reject the distortion of those laws to cover sexual preference, and we endorse the Defense of Marriage Act to prevent states from being forced to recognize same-sex unions.

Our agenda … passed the passed the Defense of Marriage Act, which defines "marriage" for purposes of federal law as the legal union of one man and one woman and prevents federal judges and bureaucrats from forcing states to recognize other living arrangements as "marriages."

2000

Taxes And Budget: Render to Caesar, But Let The People Keep Their Own

The federal tax code is dysfunctional. It penalizes hard work, marriage, thrift, and success - the very factors that are the foundations for lasting prosperity.

Children At Risk

We renew our call for replacing "family planning" programs for teens with increased funding for abstinence education, which teaches abstinence until marriage as the responsible and expected standard of behavior. Abstinence from sexual activity is the only protection that is 100 percent effective against out-of-wedlock pregnancies and sexually transmitted diseases, including HIV/AIDS, when transmitted sexually. We oppose school-based clinics that provide referrals, counseling, and related services for contraception and abortion. We urge the states to enforce laws against statutory rape, which accounts for an enormous portion of teen pregnancy. ... Because so many social ills plaguing America are fueled by the absence of fathers, we support initiatives that strengthen marriage rates and promote committed fatherhood.

We support the traditional definition of "marriage" as the legal union of one man and one woman, and we believe that federal judges and bureaucrats should not force states to recognize other living arrangements as marriages. We rely on the home, as did the founders of the American Republic, to instill the virtues that sustain democracy itself. That belief led Congress to enact the Defense of Marriage Act, which a Republican

Department of Justice will energetically defend in the courts. For the same reason, we do not believe sexual preference should be given special legal protection or standing in law. We will protect the rights of families in international programs and will not fund organizations involved in abortion. This approach to foreign assistance will unify people, respect their diverse beliefs, and uphold basic human rights. It will enable us, in cooperation with other free societies around the world, to more effectively oppose religious persecution and the sex trafficking that ruins the lives of women and children.

2004

The sound principle of judicial review has turned into an intolerable presumption of judicial supremacy. A Republican Congress, working with a Republican president, will restore the separation of powers and re-establish a government of law. There are different ways to achieve that goal, such as using Article III of the Constitution to limit federal court jurisdiction.

Protecting Marriage
We strongly support President Bush's call for a Constitutional amendment that fully protects marriage, and we believe that

neither federal nor state judges nor bureaucrats should force states to recognize other living arrangements as equivalent to marriage. We believe, and the social science confirms, that the well-being of children is best accomplished in the environment of the home, nurtured by their mother and father anchored by the bonds of marriage. We further believe that legal recognition and the accompanying benefits afforded couples should be preserved for that unique and special union of one man and one woman which has historically been called marriage.

After more than two centuries of American jurisprudence, and millennia of human experience, a few judges and local authorities are presuming to change the most fundamental institution of civilization, the union of a man and a woman in marriage. Attempts to redefine marriage in a single state or city could have serious consequences throughout the country, and anything less than a Constitutional amendment, passed by the Congress and ratified by the states, is vulnerable to being overturned by activist judges. On a matter of such importance, the voice of the people must be heard. The Constitutional amendment process guarantees that the final decision will rest with the American people and their elected representatives. President Bush will also vigorously defend the Defense of

Marriage Act, which was supported by both parties and passed by 85 votes in the Senate. This common sense law reaffirms the right of states not to recognize same-sex marriages licensed in other states.

President Bush said, "We will not stand for judges who undermine democracy by legislating from the bench and try to remake America by court order." The Republican House of Representatives has responded to this challenge by passing H.R. 3313, a bill to withdraw jurisdiction from the federal courts over the Defense of Marriage Act. We urge Congress to use its Article III power to enact this into law, so that activist federal judges cannot force 49 other states to approve and recognize Massachusetts' attempt to redefine marriage.

2008

Sovereign American Leadership in International Organizations

Because the UN has no mandate to promote radical social engineering, any effort to address global social problems must respect the fundamental institutions of marriage and family. We assert the rights of families in all international programs and will not fund organizations involved in abortion. We strongly support the long-held policy of the Republican Party known as the "Mexico City policy," which prohibits federal monies from being given to non-governmental organizations that provide abortions or actively promote abortion as a method of family planning in other countries. We reject any treaty or agreement that would violate those values.

Preserving Traditional Marriage

Because our children's future is best preserved within the traditional understanding of marriage, we call for a constitutional amendment that fully protects marriage as a union of a man and a woman, so that judges cannot make other arrangements equivalent to it. In the absence of a national amendment, we support the right of the people of the various states to affirm traditional marriage through state initiatives. Republicans recognize the importance of having in the home a father and a mother who are married. The two-parent family still provides the best environment of stability, discipline, responsibility, and character. Children in homes without fathers are more likely to commit a crime, drop out of school, become violent, become teen parents, use illegal drugs, become mired in poverty, or have emotional or behavioral problems. We support the courageous efforts of single-parent families to provide a stable home for their children. Children are our nation's most precious resource. We also salute and support the efforts of foster and adoptive families.

Republicans have been at the forefront of protecting traditional marriage laws, both in the states and in Congress. A Republican Congress enacted the Defense of Marriage Act, affirming the right of states not to recognize same-sex "marriages" licensed in other states.

2012

Defending Marriage Against An Activist Judiciary
A serious threat to our country's constitutional order, perhaps even more dangerous than presidential malfeasance, is an activist judiciary, in which some judges usurp the powers reserved to other branches of government. A blatant example has been the court-ordered redefinition of marriage in several States. This is more than a matter of warring legal concepts and ideals. It is an assault on the foundations of our society, challenging the institution which, for thousands of years in

virtually every civilization, has been entrusted with the rearing of children and the transmission of cultural values.

Judicial Activism: A Threat to the U.S. Constitution

Despite improvements as a result of Republican nominations to the judiciary, some judges in the federal courts remain far afield from their constitutional limitations. The U.S. Constitution is the law of the land. Judicial activism which includes reliance on foreign law or unratified treaties undermines American law. The sole solution, apart from impeachment, is the appointment of constitutionalist jurists, who will interpret the law as it was originally intended rather than make it. That is both a presidential responsibility, in selecting judicial candidates, and a senatorial responsibility, in confirming them. We urge Republican Senators to do all in their power to prevent the elevation of additional leftist ideologues to the courts, particularly in the waning days of the current Administration.

Preserving and Protecting Traditional Marriage

The institution of marriage is the foundation of civil society. Its success as an institution will determine our success as a nation. It has been proven by both experience and endless social science studies that traditional marriage is best for children. Children raised in intact married families are more likely to attend college, are physically and emotionally healthier, are less likely to use drugs or alcohol, engage in crime, or get pregnant outside of marriage. The lack of family formation not only leads to more government costs, but also to more government control over the lives of its citizens in all aspects. We recognize and honor the courageous efforts of those who bear the many burdens of parenting alone, even as we believe that marriage, the union of one man and one woman must be upheld as the national standard, a goal to stand for, encourage, and promote through laws governing marriage. We embrace the principle that all Americans should be treated with respect and dignity.

A Sacred Contract: Defense of Marriage

That is why Congressional Republicans took the lead in enacting the Defense of Marriage Act, affirming the right of States and the federal government not to recognize same-sex relationships licensed in other jurisdictions. The current Administration's open defiance of this constitutional principle—in its handling of immigration cases, in federal personnel benefits, in allowing a same-sex marriage at a military base, and in refusing to defend DOMA in the courts—makes a mockery of the President's inaugural oath. We commend the United States House of Representatives and State Attorneys General who have defended these laws when they have been attacked in the courts. We reaffirm our support for a Constitutional amendment defining marriage as the union of one man and one woman. We applaud the citizens of the majority of States which have enshrined in their constitutions the traditional concept of marriage, and we support the campaigns underway in several other States to do so.

Appendix C
We Believe in America
2012 Republican Platform (excerpts)

The First Amendment: The Foresight of Our Founders to Protect Religious Freedom

The first provision of the First Amendment concerns freedom of religion. That guarantee reflected Thomas Jefferson's Virginia Statute for Religious Freedom, which declared that no one should "suffer on account of his religious opinion or belief, but that all men shall be free to profess, and by argument to maintain, their opinion in matters of religion." That assurance has never been more needed than it is today, as liberal elites try to drive religious beliefs—and religious believers—out of the public square. The Founders of the American Republic universally agree that democracy presupposes a moral people and that, in the words of George Washington's Farewell Address, "Of all the dispositions and habits which lead to political prosperity, religion and morality are indispensable supports."

The most offensive instance of this war on religion has been the current Administration's attempt to compel faith-related institutions, as well as believing individuals, to contravene their deeply held religious, moral, or ethical beliefs regarding health services, traditional marriage, or abortion. This forcible secularization of religious and religiously affiliated organizations, including faith-based hospitals and colleges, has been in tandem with the current Administration's audacity in declaring which faith related activities are, or are not, protected by the First Amendment—an unprecedented aggression repudiated by a unanimous Supreme Court in its *Hosanna Tabor v. EEOC decision.*

We pledge to respect the religious beliefs and rights of conscience of all Americans and to safeguard the independence of their institutions from government. We support the public display of the Ten Commandments as a reflection of our history and of our country's Judeo-Christian heritage, and we affirm the right of students to engage in prayer at public school events in public schools and to have equal access to public schools and other public facilities to accommodate religious freedom in the public square. We assert every citizen's right to apply religious values to public policy and the right of faith-based organizations to participate fully in public programs without renouncing their beliefs, removing religious symbols, or submitting to government-imposed hiring practices. We oppose government discrimination against businesses due to religious views. We support the First Amendment right of freedom of association of the Boy Scouts of America and other service organizations whose values are under assault.

The Current Administration's Failure: Leading From Behind

The Republican Party is the advocate for a strong national defense as the pathway to peace, economic prosperity, and the protection of those yearning to be free. Since the end of World War II, American military superiority has been the cornerstone of a strategy that seeks to deter aggression or defeat those who threaten our national security interests. In 1981, President Reagan came to office with an agenda of strong American leadership, beginning with a restoration of our country's military strength. The rest is history, written in the rubble of the Berlin Wall and the Iron Curtain. We face a similar challenge today.

Conventional Forces in Decline

More than a century ago, Republican President Theodore Roosevelt predicted that America's future was in the Pacific. That future is here today, but it can develop peacefully only under the shield of American Naval and Air power. Yet the current Administration plans to significantly curtail production of our most advanced combat aircraft, decommission 6 of 60 Air Force tactical squadrons, and eliminate critical air mobility assets, including 27 giant C-5As and 65 C-130s, while divesting the nation of the brand new C-27. The President plans to reduce our naval forces by retiring seven cruisers and slowing work on amphibious ships and attack submarines, further reducing the Navy that already has the smallest fleet since the early years of the twentieth century. And he will reduce ground forces by separating 100,000 soldiers and Marines—many of whom will be discharged after recently returning from combat—and another 100,000 under the sequester. These plans limit our strategic flexibility in an increasingly dangerous world. The current President is repeating the disastrous cuts of the post-Vietnam war era, putting our nation in danger of returning to the "hollow force" of the Carter Administration, when the U.S. military was not respected in the world.

Nuclear Forces and Missile Defense Imperiled

We recognize that the gravest terror threat we face—a nuclear attack made possible by nuclear proliferation—requires a comprehensive strategy for reducing the world's nuclear stockpiles and preventing the spread of those armaments. But the U.S. can lead that effort only if it maintains an effective strategic arsenal at a level sufficient to fulfill its deterrent purposes, a notable failure of the current Administration. The United States is the only nuclear power not modernizing its nuclear stockpile. It took the current Administration just one year to renege on the President's commitment to modernize the neglected infrastructure of the nuclear weapons complex—a commitment made in exchange for approval of the New START treaty. The current Administration has systematically undermined America's missile defense, abandoning the missile defense bases in Poland and the Czech Republic, reducing the number of planned interceptors in Alaska, and cutting the budget for missile defense. In an embarrassing open microphone discussion with former Russian President

Medvedev, the current President made clear that, if he wins a second term, he intends to exercise "more flexibility" to appease Russia, which means further undermining our missile defense capabilities. ...

An America That Leads: The Republican National Security Strategy for the Future

We will honor President Reagan's legacy of peace through strength by advancing the most cost-effective programs and policies crucial to our national security, including our economic security and fiscal solvency. To do that, we must honestly assess the threats facing this country, and we must be able to articulate candidly to the American people our priorities for the use of taxpayer dollars to address those threats. We must deter any adversary who would attack us or use terror as a tool of government. Every potential enemy must have no doubt that our capabilities, our commitment, and our will to defeat them are clear, unwavering, and unequivocal. We must immediately employ a new blueprint for a National Military Strategy that is based on an informed and validated assessment of the potential threats we face, one that restores as a principal objective the deterrence using the full spectrum of our military capabilities. As Ronald Reagan proved by the victorious conclusion of the Cold War, only our capability to wield overwhelming military power can truly deter the enemies of the United States from threatening our people and our national interests. In order to deter aggression from nation-states, we must maintain military and technical superiority through innovation while upgrading legacy systems including aircraft and armored vehicles. ... We will accept no arms control agreement that limits our right to self-defense; and we will fully deploy a missile defense shield for the people of the United States and for our allies. We will pursue an effective cybersecurity strategy, supported by the necessary resources, that recognizes the importance of offensive capabilities.

Appendix D
Resolutions Passed by the
Republican National Committee

Pro-Life

2013

RESOLUTION SUPPORTING RELIGIOUS FREEDOM AND HOBBY LOBBY

WHEREAS, A Health and Human Services regulation promulgated to enable "The Affordable Care Act of 2010" also known as "Obamacare" now demands that employers pay for the contraceptive methods of their employees, including drugs that cause abortion; and

WHEREAS, these abortifacients violate the first "unalienable right," the right to life (written in the Declaration of

94

Independence) with which all human beings are endowed by their Creator and which is a preeminent tenet of Judeo-Christian religions; and

WHEREAS, Hobby Lobby, the craft store giant, operating over 500 stores in 42 states and employing over 13,000 full-time employees eligible for health care, will be forced to pay for insurance coverage that violates the religious principles held by owner, founder, and CEO David Green; and

WHEREAS, Hobby Lobby has provided health care for employees who are eligible; however, if the store refuses to comply with this new provision it could face a $1.3 million per day in government fines; and

WHEREAS, Hobby Lobby has filed suit stating that, under the First Amendment to the Constitution, which states that Congress shall not pass laws prohibiting the free exercise of religion, the federal government does not have the authority to force a business to participate in a program that violates the business owner's religious principles; and

WHEREAS, David Green, who has operated his company since 1970 according to his religious beliefs, has stated, "we seek to honor God by operating the company in a manner consistent with Biblical principles"; therefore, be it

RESOLVED, that the Republican National Committee stands with and commends the courageous actions of Mr. Green and Hobby Lobby to defend his right to operate his company according to his strongly and consistently held traditional religious principles.

As adopted by the Republican National Committee on January 25, 2013

RESOLUTION TO REDISTRIBUTE PLANNED PARENTHOOD FUNDING

WHEREAS, Planned Parenthood's most recent annual report stated that during fiscal year 2011- 2012, Planned Parenthood received a record $542 million in taxpayer funding in the form of government grants, contracts, and Medicaid reimbursements; and

WHEREAS, Taxpayer funding consists of 45% of Planned Parenthood's annual revenue; and WHEREAS in 2011, Planned Parenthood performed a record high 333,964 abortions; and

WHEREAS, over the past three reported years (2009-2011), Planned Parenthood has performed nearly one million abortions (995,687); and

WHEREAS, in 2011, abortions made up 92% of Planned Parenthood's pregnancy services, while prenatal care and adoption referrals accounted for only 7% (28,674) and 0.6% (2,300), respectively; and

WHEREAS, for every adoption referral, Planned Parenthood performed 145 abortions; and

WHEREAS, despite Planned Parenthood's claims that it offers women's healthcare services, cancer screening and prevention services provided by Planned Parenthood have dropped by 29% since 2009; and

WHEREAS, Planned Parenthood reported $87.4 million in excess revenue, and more than $1.2 billion in net assets; therefore, be it

RESOLVED, that the Republican National Committee calls upon Democrats and Republicans in Congress and the President to ensure that women do not suffer from lack of cancer screening and preventative services, by directing that such amounts as are currently being used by Planned Parenthood for screening will be diverted to organizations that specialize in cancer screening for women and who have not cut back on those services.

As adopted by the Republican National Committee on January 25, 2013

RESOLUTION SUPPORTING CORE VALUES OF THE 2012 REPUBLICAN PLATFORM

WHEREAS, the 2012 Republican Platform states, "our rights come from God, are protected by government, and that the only just government is one that truly governs with the consent of the governed," (Preamble, p. i); and

WHEREAS, the 2012 Republican Platform states, "Faithful to the "self-evident" truths enshrined in the Declaration of Independence, we assert the sanctity of human life and affirm that the unborn child has a fundamental individual right to life which cannot be infringed. We support a human life amendment to the Constitution and endorse legislation to make clear that the Fourteenth Amendment's protections apply to the unborn children" (We The People: A Restoration of the Constitution, p. 13-14); and

WHEREAS, the 2012 Republican Platform states, "We uphold the right of individuals to keep and bear arms, a right which antedated the Constitution and was solemnly confirmed by the Second Amendment" (We The People: A Restoration of Constitutional Government, p. 13); and

WHEREAS, the 2012 Republican Platform states, "We believe that marriage, the union of one man and one woman must be upheld as the national standard, a goal to stand for, encourage, and promote through laws governing marriage," and "We embrace the principle that all Americans should be treated with respect and dignity," (Renewing American Values to Build

Healthy Families, Great Schools and Safe Neighborhoods, p. 31); and

WHEREAS, the 2012 Republican Platform states, "The greatest asset of the American economy is the American worker," and "Just as immigrant labor helped build our country in the past, today's legal immigrants are making vital contributions in every aspect of our national life," and "Their industry and commitment to American values strengthens our economy, enriches our culture, and enables us to better understand and more effectively compete with the rest of the world"; and

WHEREAS, the 2012 Republican Platform further states, "Illegal immigration undermines those benefits and affects U.S. workers. In an age of terrorism, drug cartels, human trafficking, and criminal gangs, the presence of millions of unidentified persons in this country poses grave risks to the safety and the sovereignty of the United States," and "Our highest priority, therefore, is to secure the rule of law both at our borders and at ports of entry" (Reforming Government to Serve the People, p. 25); therefore be it

100

RESOLVED, the Republican National Committee reaffirms our commitment to the core values of the Republican Party as stated in the 2012 Republican Platform approved by the delegates to the Republican National Convention on August 28, 2012.

As adopted by the Republican National Committee on April 12, 2013

2014

RESOLUTION ON REPUBLICAN PRO-LIFE STRATEGY

WHEREAS, The Democrats have waged a deceptive "War on Women" attack against Republican pro-life candidates, demonizing them and manipulating American voters; and

WHEREAS, The Republican Party is proud to stand up for the rights of the unborn and believe all Americans have an unalienable right to life as stated in The Declaration of Independence; and

WHEREAS, Pro-life Republicans should fight back

against deceptive rhetoric regardless of those in the Republican Party who encourage them to stay silent; and

WHEREAS, Candidates who stay silent on pro-life issues do not identify with key voters, fail to alert voters to the Democrats' extreme pro-abortion stances, and have lost their elections; and

WHEREAS, According to the extensive polling conducted by Gallup since 1975, many Republican stances regarding abortion garner at least 60 % support from the public and across the political spectrum:

- 87% support informed-consent laws about certain possible risks of the abortion
- 80% support banning abortion during the 3rd trimester;
- 71% support parental consent laws;
- 69% support imposing a 24-hour wait period before an abortion procedure;
- 64% of Americans support banning abortion during the 2nd trimester;
- 64% support banning partial-birth abortion;
- 64% support spousal notification laws that require the husband to be simply notified if his wife seeks an

abortion; and

WHEREAS, Staying silent fails because this strategy allows Democrats to define the Republican brand and prevents the Republican Party from taking advantage of widely supported pro-life positions listed above to attract traditional and new values voters; and

WHEREAS, Staying silent fails to alert voters to the Democrats' extreme pro-abortion stances, which voters are repelled by; therefore be it

RESOLVED, The Republican National Committee condemns the Democrats' deceptive "war on women" rhetoric;

RESOLVED, The Republican National Committee will support Republican pro-life candidates who fight back against Democratic deceptive "war on women" rhetoric by pointing out the extreme positions on abortion held by Democratic opponents;

RESOLVED, The Republican National Committee will not support the strategy of Republican pro-life candidates staying silent in the face of such deceptive rhetoric; and,

RESOLVED, The Republican National Committee urges all Republican pro-life candidates, consultants, and other national Republican Political Action Committees to reject a strategy of silence on the abortion issue when candidates are attacked with "war on women" rhetoric.

As adopted by the Republican National Committee on January 24, 2014

2015

RESOLUTION TO DEFUND PLANNED PARENTHOOD AND PREVENT THE USE OF ILLEGALLY OR UNETHICALLY OBTAINED FETAL TISSUE IN RESEARCH

WHEREAS, In the 1984 *National Organ Transplant Act*, Congress criminalized the buying and selling of organs for profit so that organizations would not profit by the sale of human organs for transplant, intentionally making the sale of human organs illegal in the United States; and

WHEREAS, Senior medical officers of Planned Parenthood were seen in recent videos negotiating prices for fetal organs and tissue in violation of these laws that prevent the sale of human tissue, and human organs and tissues can come only from human beings; and

WHEREAS, The human beings killed by abortion cannot give consent for the donation of their organs, so it is not possible to ethically obtain fetal tissue through an elective abortion; and

WHEREAS, Senior medical officers of Planned Parenthood discussed how they would alter the abortion procedure to retrieve these fetal organs and tissue in violation of the law that requires an abortion to be performed in such a way as to ensure the mother's safety only; and

WHEREAS, Planned Parenthood receives more than $500 million in taxpayer money every year; therefore be it

RESOLVED, That the Republican National Committee requests that Congress pass the *No Taxpayer Funding for Abortion and Abortion Insurance Full Disclosure Act (S. 582)* to enact a permanent, government-wide prohibition of taxpayer funding for abortion to ensure that taxpayer money is never used for the killing of innocent life or the sale of body parts of aborted babies;

RESOLVED, That the Republican National Committee calls on all branches of the United States government, including the National Institutes of Health, and State Governments to cease funding the use in research of these illegally and/or unethically obtained human organs and tissues obtained through elective abortions;

RESOLVED, That the Republican National Committee urges relevant law enforcement agencies to prosecute the employees of Planned Parenthood who profited personally or for their organizations from the sale of human organs; and

RESOLVED, That the Republican National Committee insists that Congress specifically defund Planned Parenthood immediately to make it clear that such unlawful behavior in violation of human dignity cannot be condoned.

As adopted by the Republican National Committee on August 10, 2015

<u>Pro-Family</u>

2013

RESOLUTION FOR MARRIAGE AND CHILDREN 2013

WHEREAS, the institution of marriage is the solid foundation upon which our society is built and in which children thrive; and it is based on the relationship that only a man and a woman can form; and

WHEREAS, support for marriage has been repeatedly affirmed nationally in the 2012 Republican National Platform, through the enactment of the Defense of Marriage Act in 1996 (signed into law by President Bill Clinton), and passed by the voters of 41 States including California via Proposition 8 in 2008; and

WHEREAS, no Act of human government can change the reality that marriage is a natural and most desirable union; especially when procreation is a goal; and

WHEREAS, the future of our country is children; it has been proven repeatedly that the most secure and nurturing environment in which to raise healthy well-adjusted children is in a home where both mother and father are bound together in a loving marriage; and

WHEREAS, the U. S. Supreme Court is considering the constitutionality of laws adopted to protect marriage from the unfounded accusation that support for marriage is based only on irrational prejudice against homosexuals; therefore be it

RESOLVED, the Republican National Committee affirms its support for marriage as the union of one man and one woman, and as the optimum environment in which to raise healthy children for the future of America; and be it further

RESOLVED, the Republican National Committee implores the U. S. Supreme Court to uphold the sanctity of marriage in its rulings on California's Proposition 8 and the Federal Defense of Marriage Act.

As adopted by the Republican National Committee
on April 12, 2013

RESOLUTION DEFENDING TRADITIONAL MARRIAGE

WHEREAS, the institution of marriage is the solid rock upon which our society is built and in which families thrive; and

WHEREAS, the future of our country is its children; and it has been proven both historically and scientifically that the most secure and nurturing environment in which to raise healthy well-adjusted children is in a home where both mother and father are bound together in a loving traditional marriage; and

WHEREAS, an overwhelming majority of states currently prohibit persons of the same gender from marrying, most of which have done so in their state constitutions, including the State of North Carolina which this May 8, 2012 approved such a constitutional amendment by a 20-point margin; and

WHEREAS, President Barack Obama recently announced his opposition to traditional marriage; and

WHEREAS, support for traditional marriage was affirmed nationally through the enactment of the Defense of Marriage Act in 1996, signed into law by President Bill Clinton; and

WHEREAS, President Barack Obama has directed his own Justice Department to ignore the law and to not defend DOMA; and

WHEREAS, while the RNC recognizes that families take many forms, the institution of marriage itself is sacred and its traditional form must be upheld as a national model; a goal to strive for, encourage, and promote; therefore be it

RESOLVED, the Republican National Committee affirms its support for traditional marriage as the union of one man and one woman, as expressed in the provisions of the 2008 Republican Party Platform, the 2012 Republican Party Platform draft*, and the Federal Defense of Marriage Act. *draft to be determined prior to passage of this resolution

*As adopted by the Committee on Resolutions
on August 22, 2012*

2014

RESOLUTION ON PAIN-CAPABLE UNBORN CHILD PROTECTION LAWS

WHEREAS, Republicans have championed the sanctity of human life in our National Party Platform for nearly four decades; and

WHEREAS, the Democratic Party has become the party of pro-abortion extremism, dropping even the wish that abortion be "rare" from their party's platform; and

WHEREAS, led by the state of Nebraska in April 2010, 14 states have now enacted versions of Pain-Capable Unborn Child Protection laws, almost always by overwhelming margins, recognizing the reality of pain in the unborn and providing legal protection for the unborn at 20 weeks (almost 5 months) of pregnancy and beyond; and

WHEREAS, on June 18, 2013, the U.S. House of Representatives voted to pass the national Pain-Capable Unborn Child Protection Act to provide legal protection for the unborn at 20 weeks of pregnancy and beyond in the United States; and

WHEREAS, as of March 18, 2014, at least 40 Republican members of the U.S. Senate have co-sponsored the companion bill to the House-passed legislation; however, the Democrats in control continue to callously approve of this barbaric practice; and

WHEREAS, substantial medical evidence confirms that the unborn child is capable of experiencing pain at least by 20 weeks, if not earlier; and

WHEREAS, public opinion polls on abortion after almost 5 months of pregnancy show that Americans believe this practice should be banned; 80 percent of Americans oppose abortion in the third trimester and 64 percent reject abortion after 12 weeks while 63 percent of women believe it should not be permitted after the point where substantial medical evidence says the unborn child can feel pain; and

WHEREAS, late-term abortion is emotionally and physically harmful to women, destructive of the ethical norms and reputation of the medical profession, and offensive to the canons of law, medicine, and society that require us to protect the weak from the strong, the powerless from the powerful; therefore be it

RESOLVED, the Republican National Committee reaffirms its core principle of the sanctity of human life in our party platform for nearly four decades, namely, that the unborn child has a fundamental individual right to life that cannot be infringed; and be it further

RESOLVED, that the Republican National Committee strongly supports federal, state, and local pain-capable unborn child legislation that bans abortions at 20 weeks (almost 5 months) of pregnancy and beyond.

As adopted by the Republican National Committee on May 9, 2014

Common Core

2013

RESOLUTION CONCERNING COMMON CORE EDUCATION STANDARDS

WHEREAS, the Common Core State Standards (CCSS) are a set of academic standards, promoted and supported by two private membership organizations, the National Governor's Association (NGA) and the Council of Chief State School Officers (CCSSO), as a method for conforming American students to uniform ("one size fits all") achievement goals to make them more competitive in a global marketplace; and

WHEREAS, the NGA and the CCSSO, received tens of millions of dollars from private third parties to advocate for and develop the CCSS strategy, subsequently created the CCSS through a process that was not subject to any freedom of information acts or other sunshine laws, and never piloted the CCSS; and

WHEREAS, even though Federal Law prohibits the federalizing of curriculum, the Obama Administration accepted the CCSS plan and used 2009 Stimulus Bill money to reward the states that were most committed to the president's CCSS agenda; but, they failed to give states, their legislatures and their citizens time to evaluate the CCSS before having to commit to them; and

WHEREAS, the NGA and CCSSO in concert with the same corporations developing the CCSS "assessments' have created new textbooks, digital media and other teaching materials aligned to the standards which must be purchased and adopted by local school districts in order that students may effectively compete on CCSS "assessments"; and

WHEREAS, the CCSS program includes federally funded testing and the collection and sharing of massive amounts of personal student and teacher data; and

WHEREAS, the CCSS effectively removes educational choice and competition since all schools and all districts must use Common Core "assessments" based on the Common Core

standards to allow all students to advance in the school system
and to advance to higher education pursuits; therefore be it

RESOLVED, the Republican National Committee, as stated in
the 2012 Republican Party Platform, "do[es] not believe in a
one size fits all approach to education and supports providing
broad education choices to parents and children at the State and
local level," (Renewing American Values to Build Healthy
Families, Great Schools and Safe Neighborhoods, p.35), which
is best based on a free-market approach to education for
students to achieve individual excellence; and be it further

RESOLVED, the Republican National Committee recognizes
the CCSS for what it is--an inappropriate overreach to
standardize and control the education of our children so they
will conform to a preconceived "normal"; and be it further

RESOLVED, that the Republican National Committee rejects
the collection of personal student data for any non-educational
purpose without the prior written consent of an adult student or
a child student's parent, and that it rejects the sharing of such
personal data, without the prior written consent of an adult
student or a child student's parent, with any person or entity

other than schools or education agencies within the state; and be it finally

RESOLVED, that the 2012 Republican Party Platform specifically states the need to repeal the numerous federal regulations which interfere with State and local control of public schools, (Renewing American Values to Build Healthy Families, Great Schools and Safe Neighborhoods, p. 36); and therefore, the Republican National Committee rejects this CCSS plan which creates and fits the country with a nationwide straitjacket on academic freedom and achievement.

As adopted by the Republican National Committee on April 12, 2013

2014

RESOLUTION COMMENDING PARENT ACTIVISTS ON ANTI-COMMON-CORE VICTORIES

WHEREAS, activist parents in five states, Indiana, Missouri, South Carolina, Oklahoma, and North Carolina, realized that their children's curriculums had been "dumbed down" by implementation of the Common Core Standards, which were never approved by their state legislatures; and

WHEREAS, these grass-roots activist parents lobbied their state legislatures to fight the political establishment to slow down or stop the implementation of the Common Core standards; and

WHEREAS, despite the huge funding advantage of those backing the standards, these parents were successful in rolling back the implementation of the Common Core Standards in their home states; and

WHEREAS, parents in other states are embroiled in the same David vs. Goliath fight to resist the federalization of education via the Common Core Standards; and

WHEREAS, these parents are reclaiming our heritage of citizen-directed government and inspiring others to enter the public square; therefore be it

RESOLVED, the Republican National Committee commends the work and spirit of the mothers, fathers, and other citizens who fought or are fighting to persuade their state executive and legislative branches to faithfully and fully resist federal intrusion into education policy-making, particularly via the Common Core Standards; and be it further

RESOLVED, that the Republican National Committee recognizes that the mothers, fathers, and other citizens engaged in this effort are, through their activism, following in the footsteps of the Founders.

As adopted by the Republican National Committee on August 8, 2014

RESOLUTION CONCERNING ADVANCED PLACEMENT U.S. HISTORY (APUSH)

WHEREAS, almost 500,000 U.S. students take the College Board's Advanced Placement U.S. History (APUSH) course each year which has traditionally been designed to present a balanced view of American history and to prepare students for college-level history courses; and

WHEREAS, the College Board (a private organization

unaccountable to the public) has recently released a new Framework for the APUSH course that reflects a radically revisionist view of American history that emphasizes negative aspects of our nation's history while omitting or minimizing positive aspects; and

WHEREAS, the Framework includes little or no discussion of the Founding Fathers, the principles of the Declaration of Independence, the religious influences on our nation's history, and many other critical topics that have always been part of the APUSH course; and

WHEREAS, the Framework excludes discussion of the U.S. military (no battles, commanders, or heroes) and omits many other individuals and events that greatly shaped our nation's history (for example, Albert Einstein, Jonas Salk, George Washington Carver, Rosa Parks, Dr. Martin Luther King, Tuskegee Airmen, the Holocaust); and

WHEREAS, the Framework presents a biased and inaccurate view of many important events in American history, including the motivations and actions of 17th-19th century settlers, American involvement in World War II, and the development

120

of and victory in the Cold War; and

WHEREAS, the Framework describes its detailed requirements as "required knowledge" for APUSH students, and the College Board admits that the APUSH examination will not test information outside this "required knowledge"; and

WHEREAS, because the Framework differs radically from almost all state history standards, so that APUSH teachers will have to ignore their state standards to prepare students for the AP examination, the Framework will essentially usurp almost all state history standards for the best and brightest history students; and

WHEREAS, the College Board is not making its sample examination available for public review, thus maintaining secrecy about what U.S. students are actually being tested on; therefore be it

RESOLVED, the Republican National Committee recommends that the College Board delay the implementation of the new APUSH Framework for at least a year, and that during that time a committee be convened to draft an APUSH Framework that is consistent both with the APUSH course's traditional mission, with state history standards, and with the desires of U.S. parents and other citizens for their students to learn the true history of their country; and be it further

RESOLVED, the Republican National Committee requests that state legislatures and the U.S. Congress investigate this matter; and be it further

RESOLVED, that the Republican National Committee request that Congress withhold any federal funding to the College Board (a private non-governmental organization) until the APUSH course and examination have been rewritten in a transparent manner to accurately reflect U.S. history without a political bias and to respect the sovereignty of state standards, and until sample examinations are made available to educators, state and local officials, and the public, as has long been the established practice; and be it finally

RESOLVED, that upon the approval of this resolution the Republican National Committee shall promptly deliver a copy of this resolution to every Republican member of Congress, all Republican candidates for Congress, and to each Republican state and territorial party office.

As adopted by the Republican National Committee
on August 8, 2014

RESOLUTION ON CONSTITUTING AMERICA - THE RETURN OF FOUNDING PRINCIPLES

WHEREAS, the founding principles of the United States are based upon and drawn from several important historic documents; and

WHEREAS, school children of the United States of America should understand the sacrifice that has been made for their God-given liberty so that a strong Constitutional Republic in the United States may be secured for future generations; therefore be it

RESOLVED, that the Republican National Committee calls upon the state legislatures in all fifty of the United States to introduce, hold hearings and favorably act on bills supporting the changing and teaching of the history - government sections of the curriculums in grades K - 12 and for the schools of the

United States America; and, be it further

RESOLVED, that U.S. schools in grades five through twelve include significant sections on: (1) The Charter of Liberties (1100 A.D.), (2) The Magna Carta, (3) The Mayflower Compact, (4) The Declaration of Independence, (5) The Northwest Ordinance, (6) The United States Constitution, (7) The Federalist Papers and the Anti-Federalist Papers, (8) The U.S. Bill of Rights, (9) The Pledge of Allegiance and the American National Anthem, and (10) The [Great Britain] Bill of Rights of 1689; and, be it further

RESOLVED, that there shall be questions included in the U.S. curriculum testing system to test students on their knowledge of these historic documents to ensure that students are effectively learning these time-honored principles in the aforementioned documents; and, be it finally

RESOLVED, that the Pledge of Allegiance be recited each school day morning, prior to the start of academic instruction, with a United States flag present before them.

RESOLUTION IN SUPPORT OF PARENTAL SCHOOL CHOICE PROGRAMS AND EDUCATION REFORM

WHEREAS, every child, regardless of zip code or their parents' income, deserves access to a quality education; and

WHEREAS, a quality education is the best path out of poverty and toward opportunity and equality; and

WHEREAS, too many children today, especially those from low-income or minority families or children with special needs, are trapped in failing schools that government has mandated they attend; and

WHEREAS, school choice programs improve the quality of education for America's students— especially those most in need—by expanding parental choice and driving market competition; and

WHEREAS, allowing parents to choose the best option for their children embraces a free-market approach, as schools will compete to offer the best quality education that fits each child's unique needs, abilities, and learning styles; and

WHEREAS, low-income students who received scholarships, including in Washington, DC, Milwaukee, New York City, and Louisiana, have consistently shown positive results as demonstrated by gold standard studies and these results include higher parental satisfaction, better performance in school, higher high school graduation rates, and higher college attendance rates; and

WHEREAS, parental school choice programs have also been shown to save taxpayers money and even improve nearby public schools through the power of competition; and

WHEREAS, President Barack Obama and Attorney General Eric Holder have worked to use the legal system to deny poor children access to the school of their choice in Louisiana and elsewhere; and

WHEREAS, Republicans in Congress have worked to defend the Opportunity Scholarship Program in Washington, DC from attacks by liberal elected officials and special interest groups; therefore be it

RESOLVED, the Republican National Committee encourages elected leaders to work with education advocates of all backgrounds and both parties to expand educational choice and combat misinformation about the true record of success of these powerful pathways toward opportunity; and be it further

RESOLVED, the Republican National Committee encourages state legislatures to create, expand, and protect school choice programs in the interest of parental empowerment and to improve all schools by fostering competition; and, be it therefore finally

RESOLVED, the Republican National Committee encourages Congress to incorporate school choice as an essential element of education policy in order to support new and existing state and local school choice policies.

As adopted by the Republican National Committee on May 9, 2014

Judges

2015

RESOLUTION AGAINST JUDICIAL OVERREACH

WHEREAS, The United States of America is the first country in recorded history founded solely in the rule of Law, not the rule of men;

WHEREAS, The United States Constitution is an inspired document that protects God-given rights by restraining all three branches of the Federal government (legislative, executive, judicial), which is necessary as stated in Federalist #15, "Why has government been instituted at all? Because the passions of men will not conform to the dictates of reason and justice, without constraint"; and

WHEREAS, The Federal government legitimately can act only in accordance with the 10th Amendment to the Constitution which states, "The powers not delegated to the United States by the Constitution, nor prohibited by it to the States, are reserved to the States respectively, or to the people"; and

WHEREAS, No court is empowered to rewrite human history, rewrite law, fabricate "rights" out of thin air, or call entitlements "rights"; and

WHEREAS, *King v. Burwell*, concerning the Affordable Care Act ("Obamacare"), June 2015, and *Obergefell v. Hodges*, concerning same-sex marriage, June 2015, are two recent examples of the Supreme Court substituting overreach for the Constitution's original intent; and

WHEREAS, In Federalist #78 Hamilton *incorrectly* predicted that "the judiciary, from the nature of its functions, will always be the least dangerous to the political rights of the Constitution; because it will be least in a capacity to annoy or injure them"; and

WHEREAS, Federalist #78 warns us: "It can be of no weight to say that the courts, on the pretense of a repugnancy, may substitute their own pleasure to the constitutional intentions of the legislature … the courts must declare the sense of the law; and if they should be disposed to exercise will instead of judgment, the consequence would equally be the substitution of their pleasure to that of the legislative body"; and

WHEREAS, The Declaration of Independence states that governments derive "their just powers from the consent of the governed"; therefore be it

RESOLVED, That the Republican National Committee never consented to be governed by judicial overreach, and calls on all supporters of the Constitution to join in vocal protest; and

RESOLVED, That the Republican National Committee urges Congress to pass appropriate laws to protect rights of conscience; and

RESOLVED, That the Republican National Committee insists that the next Republican President appoints judges at all Federal levels who are proven to faithfully apply the Constitution strictly according to original intent and who pledge to be servants of the law, not makers of law.

As adopted by the Republican National Committee on August 10, 2015

ABOUT THE AUTHOR

Phyllis Schlafly has been a national leader of the conservative movement since the publication of her best-selling 1964 book, *A Choice Not An Echo* which was updated and re-issued in 2014. She has been a leader of the pro-family movement since 1972, when she started her national volunteer organization called Eagle Forum. The *Ladies' Home Journal* named her one of the 100 most important women of the 20th century.

Mrs. Schlafly is the author or editor of 25 books and served as a member of the Commission on the Bicentennial of the U.S. Constitution, 1985-1991, appointed by President Reagan. She has testified before more than 50 Congressional and State Legislative committees on constitutional, national defense, and family issues.

Phyllis Schlafly is America's best-known advocate of the dignity and honor that we as a society owe to the role of fulltime homemaker. The mother of six children, she was the 1992 Illinois Mother of the Year.